CACTUS

DISCOVER THE COOLEST PLANTS OF THE DESERT

HELLO THERE, EXPLORER!

Did you know that the desert is not just sand and sun?

It's home to some of the coolest, weirdest, and spikiest plants on the planet, the cactus family!

In this book, you'll meet some amazing cactus friends who live in the dry, sunny deserts.

Some are tall like towers, some are round like balls, and some look like they're straight out of a storybook!

They may not talk, but each one has a wild way of surviving in the heat.

So grab your water bottle, put on your explorer hat, and get ready to meet the superstars of the desert — one prickly plant at a time!

1

SAGUARO

(Carnegiea gigantea)

/səˈ(g)wärō/

Meet the Saguaro, the tallest cactus in the desert!

It stands like a green tree with arms stretched to the sky, and some grow taller than a two-story house.

This mighty cactus wears a crown of white flowers in spring and becomes a cozy home for birds like owls and woodpeckers, who nest right inside its trunk.

DID YOU KNOW?

The Saguaro's flowers are Arizona's state flower!

Each flower only lasts one day, opening at night and closing by afternoon.

After blooming, the flowers turn into red fruit, which desert animals love to eat.

Little birds
like Gila
woodpeckers
and elf owls
make cozy
homes inside
holes they
carve into
this cactus!

A full-grown
Saguaro can
hold over 100
gallons of
water inside its
body. That's
like carrying a
whole bathtub
full of water!

ONE-ARMED SAGUAROS

Each Saguaro grows at its own pace — and depending on water, weather, and age, it might grow one arm, many arms, or sometimes... none at all!

A Saguaro usually doesn't even start growing arms until it's around 50 to 70 years old.

So if you see a tall cactus with just one arm, give it a wave — it's probably just getting started!

The Saguaro cactus has sharp spines that not only protect it from animals but also help keep it cool by casting tiny shadows on its skin.

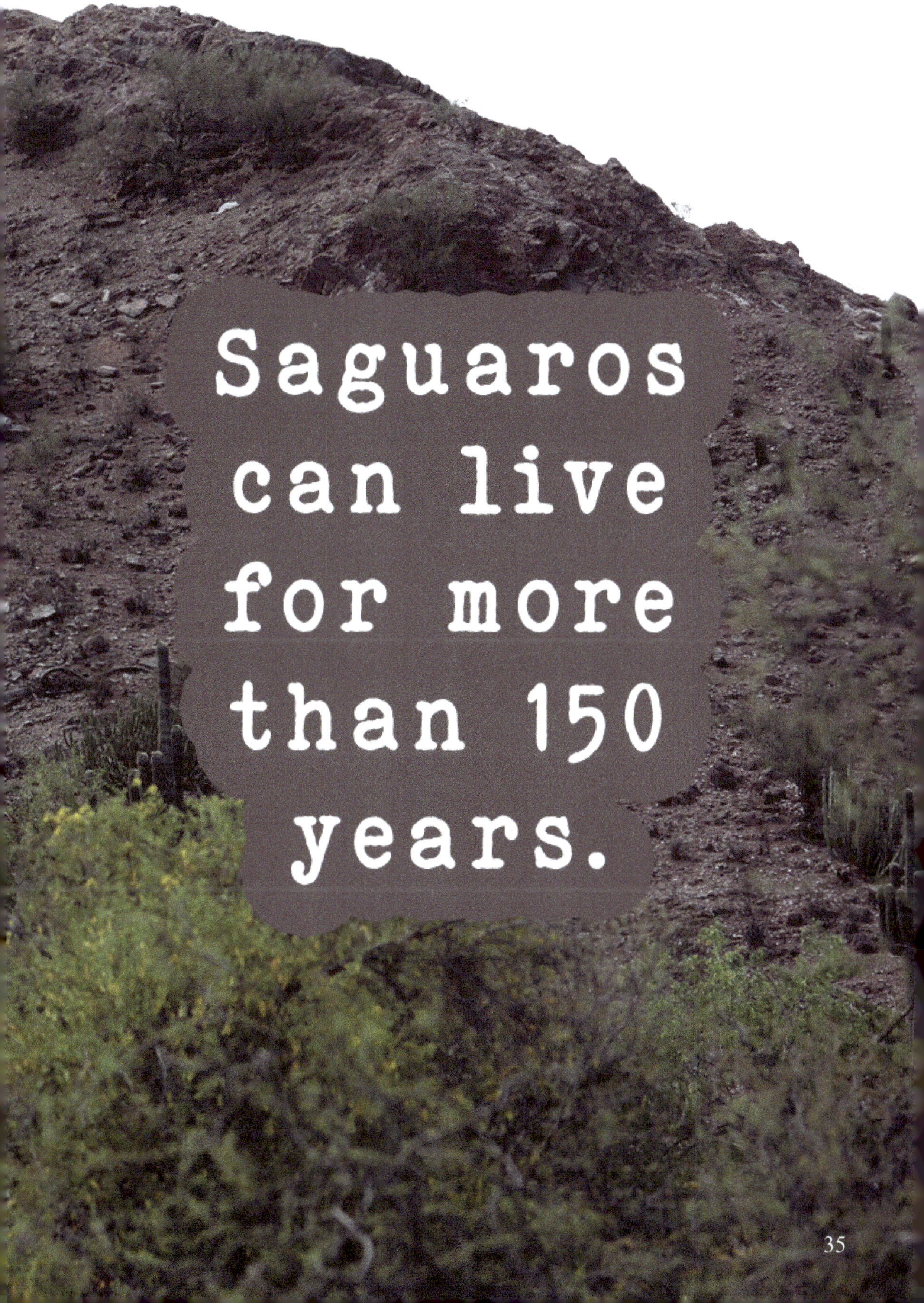

Saguaros can live for more than 150 years.

2

PRICKLY PEAR

(Opuntia)

/ˌprik(ə)lē ˈper/

The Prickly Pear looks like it's growing green bunny ears or flat pancakes!

Instead of big sharp thorns, it's covered in tiny fuzzy dots called glochids — but don't touch them, they can still poke you!

Some Prickly Pears bloom with bright yellow, orange, or pink flowers during the spring.

DID YOU KNOW?

Prickly Pears help animals too?

Their pads and fruit provide food and shelter for desert creatures like tortoises, birds, and insects.

Prickly Pear fruits are called tunas and are not only edible, but are also used to make jelly, candy, and even juice.

The pads of the Prickly Pear are sometimes called nopales, and people in Mexico cook and eat them like a vegetable.

3

BARREL CACTUS
(Ferocactus, Echinocactus)

Cactaceae   Cactus Family

Echinocactus platyacanthus

Giant Barrel Cactus
Special Protection

N to Central
Mexico   spring-summer

The Barrel Cactus is short, round, and ribbed—like a big green watermelon covered in long, sharp spines.

It can grow over 3 feet tall and live for more than 100 years!

DID YOU KNOW?

The Barrel Cactus always leans toward the southwest as it ages? It's like the plant has a built-in compass!

Cactaceae   Cactus Family

Echinocactus platyacanthus

Giant Barrel Cactus
Special Protection

N to Central
Mexico   spring-summer

Its nickname is "Compass Cactus" because people once used it to find direction.

Some Barrel Cactus species can grow flowers in a perfect circle right on top of their heads.

Desert animals like pack rats and tortoises may chew on it for moisture when water is hard to find.

The Barrel Cactus can store so much water that it swells up like a sponge during rainy seasons.

4

TEDDY BEAR CHOLLA
(Cylindropuntia bigelovii)

The Teddy
Bear Cholla
looks soft
and
fuzzy—but
it's one
desert hug
you'll
instantly
regret!

DID YOU KNOW?

The Teddy Bear Cholla's spines are so sharp and barbed that they can latch onto anything—earning it the nickname "Jumping Cholla" because it seems to leap at you!

The Teddy Bear Cholla doesn't rely on seeds alone—its spiny segments easily break off and root in the ground, allowing it to clone itself and spread across the desert like a spiky army!

5

SAN PEDRO

(Trichocereus macrogonus var. pachanoi)

The San Pedro cactus, a tall and fast-growing columnar cactus native to the Andes, has been revered for centuries for both its beauty and its traditional spiritual uses.

DID YOU KNOW?

The San Pedro cactus has been used in Andean traditional medicine and spiritual ceremonies for over 3,000 years, not just for its healing properties—but also for its powerful, naturally occurring psychedelic compound, mescaline.

The San Pedro cactus grows impressively fast for a cactus, reaching up to 12 inches (30 cm) per year, making it one of the fastest growing columnar cacti in the world.

6

CRESTED WHORTLEBERRY CACTUS
(Myrtillocactus geometrizans f. cristata)

Myrtillocactus geometrizans
frm. cristata
Crested Whortleberry Cactus

The Crested Whortleberry Cactus, is a stunning, fan-shaped mutation of the whortleberry cactus, native to central Mexico and prized by collectors for its unique, sculptural form.

DID YOU KNOW?

The "crested" shape happens when the cactus's main growing point mutates, causing it to fan out instead of growing in a single column.

The Crested Whortleberry Cactus produces small, delicate white flowers that bloom along its twisted ridges, adding a soft contrast to its dramatic, sculptural form.

This cactus is highly sought after in ornamental gardening because no two crests grow exactly the same, making each plant a one-of-a-kind living sculpture.

6

SILVER TORCH CACTUS

(Cleistocactus strausii)

The Silver Torch Cactus stands tall and slender, cloaked in a shimmering coat of white spines that glisten under the desert sun.

DID YOU KNOW?

Despite its fuzzy appearance, the Silver Torch is covered in sharp spines—its woolly look is actually a clever sunshield!

MEET THE CACTUS WREN

A clever desert bird that builds its football-shaped nests deep within the spiny arms of cacti, using the sharp spines as a natural fortress against predators.

THREATS TO CACTI

HABITAT LOSS

Many cacti lose their natural homes due to urban expansion, farming, and mining activities.

This reduces the areas where they can grow and thrive.

ILLEGAL COLLECTION

Some rare and unique cacti are taken from the wild by plant poachers who sell them in the ornamental plant trade, which can harm wild populations.

INVASIVE SPECIES

Non-native plants such as buffelgrass compete with young cactus seedlings for space, sunlight, and water, making it harder for them to survive.

This photo shows native desert plants, not buffelgrass

OVERGRAZING

Livestock and some wild animals can trample or eat young cacti, preventing them from reaching maturity.

If you have any questions,
suggestions, or feedback, we'd
love to hear from you.

Contact us at:
info@shoebill.com

www.ingramcontent.com/pod-product-compliance
Lightning Source LLC
Chambersburg PA
CBHW050241290326

41930CB00044B/3390